** Tangled In Me **
a book of messy thoughts

To all of my lovely readers, I wrote this book for you. Each word, each space, each page, placed strategically to reach the deepest and darkest parts of you that you keep so hidden. I write from my soul, but also from yours. I write about you and your silence, your pain and your happiness. I use the word 'she' to describe you, him, her, and myself. This is a book for you, about you. A book for me, about me. I hope that through these pages, words are pulled from your heart that you did not know existed, to make you feel the things you did not know you felt.

My lovely readers, may this book remind you how beautiful it is to feel.

Love always,

-JK

Special Acknowledgements:

To Annie, someone I look up to immensely. Thank you.

To my mom and dad who have carried me through life. Thank you.

To Haley, Kathryn, and Mary whose encouragement and friendship made this book possible. Thank you.

Inside of this book you will find pieces of me through words I've never said out loud. I have shed light on my shadows, erasing them with my own sunshine. Join me in both my hurt and my rejoicing. If you can not feel what I have felt, then I have failed. You owe me nothing, but because you hold this book in your hands, I owe you everything. Thank you.
This book is a written version of my heart, I hope you take care of both.

thank you for coming, i hope you choose to stay.

** Tangled In Me **
a book of messy thoughts

i would tell you to come in
and take a seat
that my heart welcomes you
but we both know
that you have already been here
since the moment i first met you
for my heart does not have doors
or time limits
locks or exit signs
it welcomes all people
in hopes that when they leave
they can look at this world
a little bit differently

I don't think we meet people by accident. Our lines are too intertwined and intricate for our paths to be crossed unintentionally.

it was a Sunday afternoon
when he asked me about my future
i told him i wanted to get a degree
and start a family
i told him about my dreams to help others
to start a business
i told him about my future house
the log cabin on the lake
with acres and acres of land
that my kids will grow up dreaming on
i told him about the library i will have
filled with all of the books i wrote
and my collection of pens
that will surely keep growing
it wasn't until i stopped to catch my breath
that i saw his smirk
he said to me with his dancing eyes
"i knew you wanted to be alive"

i think
the easiest way to heal your own
heart is to fill it with your own
kindness

is it too far fetched to think
that when stars fall from the sky
they land inside of you and i?

What a gift it is, to be able to see the clouds and still love the sky for its blue

when i am lost
i find the empty hallways,
and half finished journals,
undusted shelves,
and broken pencils

it is in those places that i have the best
chance at finding the rest of me

i do not care if your shoes are dirty
i still want to hear of all the places
they have taken you
for the dirtier your shoes are
the more stories you'll have to tell

do all things with softness
even when you can't

Isn't that a lovely thought?

That if we ever don't like where we are
We can just leave

The grass can only be greener
on the other side
if you built a fence

It's a never ending battle
dreaming of growing up
while fighting to stay young

at the simple mention
of a name
or a place
or a word that holds a deeper meaning
that only we understand
the poet in us relives and rewrites
every feeling we have ever felt
and after we live through it again
we find ourselves reburied in the mess
and the poet in us
writes about that too

my throat burns in memory of all of the things
i have left unsaid.

she had raindrops for eyes and
rose pedals for bones
entirely romantic but incredibly sad

i hope you live with so much intensity that it hurts your soul to not

some people
are made of
warning signs
and
red flags

but i think we're all
colorblind
for certain things

my roots are dug too deep
    into things that are
        not good for me

it's confusing the way our hearts and our minds so frequently disagree

but what if i told you
that each word you tell yourself
would be scribbled down
on a white lined piece of paper
and someday when you're older
and your daughter feels lost
you'll read her everything you wrote
as if it were addressed to her
i wonder what would fill
your white lined pages then

The trick was to watch her
when she thought no one was watching
The time she was undoubtedly her

finding poetry in everything
is such a blessing and a curse

i am drawn to
the most haunting things

i should of told you
when you dug your first hole
that my heart was not a map
and the 'X's were just scars
but the further you dug
the more dirt you brought up
so dark, and untouched
it was a newfound pain
that fascinated me
you made such a good pirate
that i too believed
somewhere down beneath
there was treasure inside of me

but see my friend,
that is where you are wrong
everything you could
ever want is already right
here at home

it's comforting to know
that i would not feel as if i am unworthy
if i had not once been worthy
and i would not know that these were bad days
if i had not once experienced better

how old were you when you decided
that in order to be loved you had to
be more
there is no such thing as more
in order to be loved you just have to
be you

there's a library inside of my head
filled with all of the books
i never got to finish
written by all of those who have
left me too soon

i don't know why they call it the past,
i have never known it stay there

i like to think
that my mess
is just drops of
wild and young
mixed poorly with
my puddles of love

There's something about the
grass under my toes
and the wind in my hair
that remind me how good
it feels to be alive.

i wrote goodbye in my favorite color
hoping it would hurt a little less
but it was just pain in a pretty shade

if you remember anything
let it be this
just because they don't ask you how you are,
or if you're okay
doesn't mean that you're not worth asking

my favorite days are the ones where i wake up
and know that today i get to try again

there is no timeline for healing
it happens every day that you let it

Whatever you do you must do
with the entirety of your soul

i like to think
that we all carry pens
ones of pretty pinks, blues and reds
and everywhere we go
we sign our names on the souls
of all the people we meet
and i like to think
that these sloppy signatures
form roads on the maps of their skin
and these roads lead them to places
that without us
they never could have been

She would never place her heart in his hands. Instead she'll plant it in every kiss, every touch, and every laugh. So much so that her heart will seep into his bones and become all that he knows.

if you don't believe in magic
how do you explain
snowflakes
and city lights
or good books and
the night sky?

Hold me in both of your hands
and read all of my words carefully
And when you finish reading
please fold over my corners
Just in case I'm worth remembering

please don't give credit to anyone else
i glued my own pages back together

leaving does not always mean losing
sometimes walking away is the
greatest gain you could ever get

If we had expiration dates,
a "best if used by"
maybe then we wouldn't be so
surprised when things turned sour

how cool is it
that there are billions and billions
of words inside of us
yet there are still some things
powerful enough to leave us speechless

i think we all have a little glow to us
the thing that lets us see with the lights off

May I always
remember
that I use to
dream
of these
happy days.

Think of all the stories we'd know
if we had only stopped to listen

I think that's one of my favorite thoughts
That at the end of all of this
we will get to reread our books from
start to finish and watch how we unfolded

To love her was to leave her because she was better off alone

if happy was a color, i think it'd look like
     clear skies on a summer night

and maybe we're not spinning out of control
but just dancing to our own chaos

Her triggers were not words, but the looks passed between the two girls as she walked in the room

"She was like the color yellow, Bright. Intense. Happy. She wore it wherever she went- in her smile and in her eyes. She sparkled even when she had no reason to, and she loved even when they didn't deserve it. She was yellow. Sweet like honey, bright like spring. She was the sun and the moon- shining both night and day. She was summer. So alive. So free. So careless. She existed. In everything she did, she existed. She had good thoughts and they radiated out of her onto everyone else. That's why I craved her presence. And besides, I have always loved the color yellow."

It's as simple and as complicated as this:
if you love yourself, you will always be home.

nothing humbles me more than
seeing this earth in its purest forms

happiness is contagious
spread yours everywhere

aren't we all just artists
creating pictures in our minds
of what we think we see?
our palettes changing from dark
to light, depending on how we feel?
and the details in our pictures
growing clearer and clearer the
longer we stay?

Shower her
with love
and affection
and watch
what she
can bloom into.

It was a Tuesday when I left,
for what I thought was a normal day
My heart was a little heavy
like there was something it wanted to say

I ignored it at first,
pushed it out of my mind
Filled my brain instead,
with words not so kind

I'm just your ordinary girl
there's not too much to love
But it was when I thought that thought
that something clicked up above

No wonder I'm always so tired
my heavy thoughts weigh me down
Somewhere along the years
I must have misplaced my crown

That Tuesday I chose to listen
the warmest thought that whole December
In the softest voice I heard it
"Be nice to me, I'm fragile, remember?"

i think some people are bathed in roses and lilacs and once you meet them, you spend the rest of your life wanting to breathe in their scent

The cold, the dark, the ugly
It's inside of me somewhere

she loved those late nights
spent chasing the darkness in
the middle of town
but tonight she just wanted
to lay down on her queen sized bed
and be proud of herself
for how far she had come

i said burgundy but you saw red
and i think that was just one of the
many differences between us
there was light in everything you did
and i so greatly envied you for that

It is in my silence
that I tell my greatest
stories.
Listen to the pauses in
between words, the things
I do not say. It is in
my silence that you will
discover me.

I felt her presence like the wind
sometimes yelling
sometimes whispering
but always there

I felt her presence like the sun
sometimes burning
sometimes hiding
but always there

i found a friend in the ocean
and comfort in her waves
the way she was never quite satisfied
always coming back
for a just a little bit more sand

You can not define me as any one thing
      I am both too much and too little
I can not be tied down to just one word

when you watch me leave do you see strength
and independence
or do you see someone who is too weak to stay

My vision is through a mirror
I only see what is already behind me
I am tangled in my past
wrapped so tight it is hard to breathe
My breath will always fog up the windows
I was not made to be clean

i often wonder
if the night sky looks down on us with the
same admiration that we have for it
like just as we are wishing on the stars
they are also wishing on us

if you could see my pain
i wonder if you would still
think of me that way

sometimes i pretend
that we are all different plants
growing in the gardens of those we love
and when we are picked to join
someone else's bouquet
we drop a seed deep into the soils
of those we have left
so even when we are gone
there will always be a piece of us
growing inside of them

and what a gift it is
to be able to exist
both when you are happy
and when you are not

i think that when i was born
i made friends with the night sky
because i feel as if i have known
these stars forever

i relate to the man on the street who buries
his head when he sees his own reflection
i too am ashamed of the things i have seen

i hope you learn to forgive yourself
for you are only this version of you
because you were once that version

you came down as rain
but landed as snowflakes
just as fascinating
but not quite the same

my heart sits on a well used welcome mat
with no exit sign
once you enter you'll stay forever

today could be your anniversary
or your daughter's birthday
the day you meet the in laws
or get your diploma
it could be the day you get promoted
or the day you buy a house
so i know it's not great right now
but the list of what this day could be
is endless
i don't know everything but i do know this
you will never know what today could be
if you don't stay to find out

don't mistake things
for your home
they could just be
the car bringing
you to your next
destination

in a world as big as this
i'm really quite small
which means the problems in my head
can hardly be seen at all

i tried to meet you
to hug you, to love you
but in order to see you
i had to climb over
massive bricks
and prickly vines
you were a master at
keeping people out
even those with the
heaviest winds
so before you tell me
that you are not strong
take a look at these
walls you've built

not all storms are deadly
i learned that when i met you
some storms are just heavy rain
and strong winds
hurricanes making room for the next best thing

Her wild kept
me entertained
But her innocence
is why I stayed

Somewhere inside of her there's a sprinkle of October. She's a little bit chilly. A little bit refreshing. She's boots and a sweater. Glasses and hot coffee. She's the colors on the trees, the breeze that knocks them down. I'm intrigued by the side of her that haunts me. She leaves faster than she comes, sometimes it's like she was never there at all. Just one month until she is gone. Two months until she starts over with someone new. Yes, she reminds me of October.

you are full of art because you are alive and
that is the most powerful work of them all

you're chaotic, bright, and busy
full of life and full of people
always on the move but with no where to go

i have never been to New York City but i like
to think that it's a little like you

She wrote love notes with her smile
and gave one to everyone she met
it was a trance you could not avoid
knowing her was loving her

i hope
i make you think
of poetry
and soft words
strawberries
and sunny days
i hope
i make you think
of all the things
that you love

Next time you are at the ocean
look out as far as you can
Those waters hold secrets
older than we can count
They have watched countless years
of life go by
they have lived through countless
years of death
Each crash against the shore
is another tale
Next time you are at the ocean
stop and listen to all the stories
it has to tell

I wrote about my darkness but my words came
out in color

Talking about it is everything

She dreamt of you for years
longed for you for months
She loved every part of you
with her whole heart
your hair, your skin, your smile
She was fascinated by every move you made
and talked about you whenever she could
And when you finally came
you entered this world so loved
I saw her tears and I knew
on this special day, she too had come to life

You tell me goodbye and hello in the same sentence and I can no longer understand the meaning of either

we were lost in the woods for hours,
i couldn't feel my face
but her being her,
she grabbed my hand and smiled
teeth chattering from the cold, she laughed
"isn't this pretty?"
i smiled as my heart exploded
her.
a million times over, i'd choose her.

Twelve months ago I was constantly hoping for something more. I was hoping for a change, I wanted something different. Twelve months ago today, I was not content with where I was at and twelve months ago today, was not enough for me. But now, I want nothing more than to go back to twelve months ago because twelve months ago today, really wasn't that bad. Looking back now, my life twelve months ago should have been enough for me, and I'm sure in twelve months I will feel the same about today. So maybe I should learn to enjoy now before it's twelve months too late and now is back then and today is already gone.

All she can do
is sit with her door unlocked
and her arms wide open
and just wait for you to come back home

i think that's the coolest thing about words
  it only takes two to make forever happen

I wish I could un-see the things I've seen
Un-hear the things I've heard
Un-feel the things I've felt
And un-know the things I've learned

Deep breaths
the silent reminder that we are in control

```
Look at the things you can not see
Only then will you realize her true beauty
```

We are all a work in progress
Rough drafts that may never be finished

I wish you would look to yourself for hope
because you are the most inspiring girl I know

```
Do not be afraid to take your mask off
I understand why it is there
But I promise you do not need it with me
```

I am so fascinated by all of
the people I have not met yet
the pages I have not turned
and the books I have not read
I am so fascinated by all of the
things I do not yet know

i think it's important
this glass half full mentality
there is always room for more
but there is no such thing as empty

You could burn down entire cities
with the fire raging inside of you
But I think that you would feel a lot
      more satisfied, if instead
You burnt down the part of you that
   longed to watch these cities fall

You ignited a spark in me that I didn't know existed
A light that I never want to stop glowing

Each tick of the clock was a reminder that time is and always will be the most consistent friend in my life

You are so content with your existence
and I admire that immensely
There is great courage in being happily alone

and that was my goal
 to not only survive
but to live as well.

it was a crazy beautiful mess
this story of her life
a mess i couldn't wait to get involved in

You are not held down
by anyone but yourself
remember that

I could write the most fascinating poem
with the prettiest words
but it still wouldn't compare
to the elegance of you

know this and know this with your whole heart
all of the happiness in this world
is held inside of you

i want to take every nightfall
and scatter the darkness around you
in hopes to prove that your dreams have always
been reachable

I changed colors with every breath I took
I was a masterpiece of the outdoors
A wild work of art

Take the step
The one that scares you
And then take another
Your footprints are worth seeing
And this growth is worth talking about

even if it meant losing her
i would still choose to love her
because loving her was teaching me
the beauty of this world

Dream in brightness but also in darkness
The colors of this life will mean
that much more to you
when the light gets turned back on

You think she is weak
for admitting that she is familiar with this
pain
but I think you are weaker
for pretending that you are not

"You"
the only word in this world where the power
behind it is held in only your hands

I have felt the world and now I want to see it

It took me years to discover
That you don't have to let things go
You're allowed to bottle up
What you'll always want to know
For example, take these mountains
Or the trails that I've been on
I would start to miss them
Before they were even gone
So instead, today I'll choose
To sit back and soak it in
I know that this is something
I'll want to enjoy again
This feeling can last forever
The one where I feel free
As long as I remember to bottle it up
And bring it back home with me

You are a gift
And that is why you force everyone
to unwrap you before you show them who you
truly are

The old man looked down at the boy and said
Oh how lucky you are to be so young
And the boy looked back at him and said
Oh how lucky you are to have witnessed so much life

Undust your soul and get back out there
This world is waiting for you

```
                          Fear
       the simple reminder that we are alive
```

when I walk through the woods
i feel the presence of the millions
    who have come before me
their souls still lost in the trees
   claiming these roots as home

To me she was not just a friend but hope wrapped in that smile she wore despite the millions of reasons she had to not

Be so proud of yourself that you're not afraid
to tell your story

I promise you
you will find it
happiness will come
and when it does
it will swallow you whole
and drown you
in all of the best ways

you will never see her tiptoeing
she knew no such thing as
existing quietly

my darling
the sun will always melt the pain away
you just have to let it

shed the parts of you that tell you
you can't do it
that you're not worth it
shed the parts of you that weigh you down
the skin that keeps you from growing

May you always be the one
who chooses to see both sides of every story

Embrace what makes you you
You are just as lovely
being twice as messy

Your life is a storybook with hundreds of chapters. Whether you reread, rewrite, or erase some from memory is all your choice. Some you will read slowly because the joy you get from these characters makes you want the chapter to never end. Others will be read so quickly that the words start to blend together. You will come to realize that there are certain chapters in your life that are not to be reopened. The purpose was fulfilled the first time around and there is no need for you to reread or dwell on what already happened. Through experience you will find that these characters caused you enough pain in the present, and no matter how many times you try to reword it, the ending will always remain the same. The characters, the theme, and the setting will change many times throughout your story. Sometimes so often and so quickly, it seems as if you started a new book.

I hope that as you read and write this book, you accept that change is good. And understand that no story can exist without the author and the main character. So keep going, keep breathing, and keep writing your story.

And my darling i promise
that if you only stopped
looking for the rain, then
the clouds would remain
beautiful even when they're
dark. and i promise that the
overgrown path will still get
you there, even if it takes
you a little longer. My darling
you must stop searching for
the bad because i promise
you'll always find it

** thank you **

Authors Note:

These words have been Tangled In Me since I was born. For the last year I have worked to lay them out on these pages perfectly so that when my readers open this book, they can feel the amount of love and care that has gone into creating it.

This page has been the hardest to write because there is no way to accurately explain how much I appreciate all of you. Whether you realized it or not, each and every reader of mine personally carried me through this process. Never does a day go by where I am not grateful for all of you. Thank you.

As always, all of my love being sent your way.

-JK

About the Author:

Jodi is a first time author who has been speaking at open mic nights and sharing her words via Instagram for years. She currently lives in Minnesota while pursuing her Bachelor's degree in Mass Communications. Jodi is a lover of adventure and all things outdoors. If she is not writing, then she is thinking about writing, and if she is not thinking about writing then she is reading. Her heart can be found in everything she lays her eyes on, for to her, this world is the most magnificent of all poetry. You can find more of her work on Instagram as @jk.writings.

all of my love

-JK

Made in the USA
San Bernardino, CA
11 April 2019